THE LETTERS TO THE SEVEN CHURCHES

A Study in Revelation 1-3

By Estrelda Alexander

Seymour Press *SP*
Capitol Heights, MD

THE LETTERS TO THE SEVEN CHURCHES

A Study in the Book of Revelation 1-3

ISBN: 978-1-938373-23-7
LCCN: 2020931582

Seymour Press
Capitol Heights, MD
All rights reserved.

TABLE OF CONTENTS

Preface

Numerous studies have been written about the book of Revelation. Many of these take either a rigidly liberal or conservative stand about the origins, purpose, and spiritual connotations of the book or have dismissed it as pure allegory with no practical application to the real world. Arguments over authorship, prophetic implications, and eschatological value have waged over the centuries but have often obscured the real value of the book for contemporary Christians.

A practical look at seven letters written to seven real first century congregations in the earliest part of the book provides an excellent example of the usefulness of the message of Revelation for today's church. In a world of social and political unrest, spiritual confusion, and ethical quandaries, what does the Spirit have to say to contemporary believers? What do these letters have to offer for everyday Christians whose faith is tested by the ordinary struggles and hard issues of life?

Specific questions arise for us from the text. What does Christ say to us about Himself? For what can He commend or condemn his Church? What spiritual correction is offered for those who are in error? What encouragement is provided to the persecuted or the disheartened? What promise does it hold for our future?

Again, these letters were written to real churches, but none remain in existence today. And, though they appear far removed from our reality, the lessons in this volume are designed to help Christians in every age discover and apply the valuable practical truths coded in their messages.

GETTING THE MOST OUT OF THIS STUDY

This Bible study is meant to be interactive. A teacher may be there to guide you, but a lot of the work will be done by you, the student.

In reading and understanding John's vision, it is helpful to appreciate the history of the cities and each church. It is also helpful to recognize the impact of Roman rule, the symbolism; and the references to people, places, and events within each letter. If as you read each scriptural passage, you come to something you don't understand, Look It Up! Start with a good Bible dictionary and commentary. A Bible atlas would also help, as would a pronunciation guide.

Read each day's devotional passages during the week before the respective session on a specific church. These will provide insight into the particular meaning and context of each church's letter. Look at each week's discussion questions before coming to class and be ready to actively participate in the discussion.

Most importantly, approach this study with an open heart and mind. Look for what the writer's words have to speak to us as Christians who are challenged to be faithful to Christ in a contemporary, unbelieving world. What does it speak to us of God's character? What commendation, encouragement, and promises can we take from it? What condemnation, warning and admonition must we pay attention to?

If you apply these simple principles you will find this to be a rewarding method of studying the Bible. And like each church is admonished, listen to hear "what the Spirit says to the Church and to each believer

INTRODUCTION: THE LETTERS TO THE SEVEN CHURCHES:
Revelation 1-3

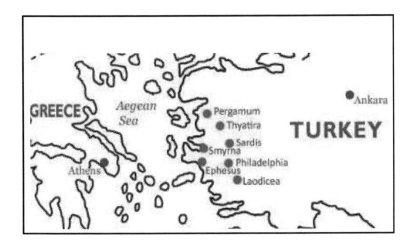

The book of Revelation, also called the Revelation of John or Apocalypse of John, is one of the only two apocalyptic texts in the Bible. The book of Daniel (Chapter 7-12) in the Old Testament is the only other apocalyptic literature in Scripture.

The authorship of the book of Revelation is under debate. Some scholars feel the writer was the beloved Apostle, but this is not a generally accepted point, especially among more liberal scholars. What we can say for sure is that the writer's name was John, and that he was probably Jewish or at least remarkably familiar with Jewish life, customs, and imagery.

The term "Apocalypse" (ἀποκάλυψις) is a Greek word meaning the "unveiling or unfolding of things previously unknown and unknowable apart from the unveiling." It refers to a type of religious writing characterized by a heavily symbolic focus on eschatology and the receiving of the revelation by an individual from a heavenly being.

This highly symbolic literature flourished for three centuries: between 200 B.C.E. and 100 C.E. It appeared during times of crisis and was intended to strengthen and encourage the faithful by conveying a message of God's sovereignty, supernatural intervention, and final triumph for those suffering hardship. Though the battle is dramatically and symbolically played out in the earthly realm, the real struggle is on a higher level, with the ultimate antagonism seen as between God and Satan.

Some commentators see the letters as a purely literary device, addressed to the church at large with seven as an artificial number. Others see the seven as standing sequentially and prophetically for stages of church history. Using this scheme, the following order is suggested:

The Seven Periods of Church History

Ephesus	Apostolic Church	33-99
Smyrna	Persecuted Church	100-313
Pergamos	Early Medieval Church	313-537
Thyatira	Late Medieval Church	538-1517
Sardis	Reformation Church	1517-1648
Philadelphia	Missionary Church	1648-1900
Laodicea	Apostatized Church	1900-present

Others interpret the letters as addressed to real churches. Each part bears relevance to what is known of existing conditions of the city named and alludes to either a feature of the host city or specific event(s) which marked that city at the time it was written.

LESSON I: OVERVIEW
Revelation 1

1 The Revelation of Jesus Christ, which God gave Him to show His servants—things which must shortly take place. And He sent and signified it by His angel to His servant John,

2 who bore witness to the word of God, and to the testimony of Jesus Christ, to all things that he saw.

3 Blessed is he who reads and those who hear the words of this prophecy, and keep those things which are written in it; for the time is near.

4 John, to the seven churches which are in Asia: Grace to you and peace from Him who is and who was and who is to come, and from the seven Spirits who are before His throne,

5 and from Jesus Christ, the faithful witness, the firstborn from the dead, and the ruler over the kings of the earth. To Him who loved us and washed us from our sins in His own blood,

6 and has made us kings and priests to His God and Father, to Him be glory and dominion forever and ever. Amen.

7 Behold, He is coming with clouds, and every eye will see Him, even they who pierced Him. And all the tribes of the earth will mourn because of Him. Even so, Amen.

8 "I am the Alpha and the Omega, the Beginning and the End," says the Lord, "who is and who was and who is to come, the Almighty."

9 I, John, both your brother and companion in the tribulation and kingdom and patience of Jesus Christ, was on the island that is called Patmos for the word of God and for the testimony of Jesus Christ.

10 I was in the Spirit on the Lord's Day, and I heard behind me a loud voice, as of a trumpet,

11 saying, "I am the Alpha and the Omega, the First and the Last," and, "What you see, write in a book and send it to the seven churches which are in Asia: to Ephesus, to Smyrna, to Pergamos, to Thyatira, to Sardis, to Philadelphia, and to Laodicea."

12 Then I turned to see the voice that spoke with me. And having turned I saw seven golden lampstands,

13 and in the midst of the seven lampstands One like the Son of Man, clothed with a garment down to the feet and girded about the chest with a golden band.

14 His head and hair were white like wool, as white as snow, and His eyes like a flame of fire;

15 His feet were like fine brass, as if refined in a furnace, and His voice as the sound of many waters;

16 He had in His right hand seven stars, out of His mouth went a sharp two-edged sword, and His countenance was like the sun shining in its strength.

17 And when I saw Him, I fell at His feet as dead. But He laid His right hand on me, saying to me, "Do not be afraid; I am the First and the Last.

18 I am He who lives, and was dead, and behold, I am alive forevermore. Amen. And I have the keys of Hades and of Death.

19 Write the things which you have seen, and the things which are, and the things which will take place after this.

20 The mystery of the seven stars which you saw in My right hand, and the seven golden lampstands: The seven stars are the angels of the seven churches, and the seven lampstands which you saw are the seven churches.

BACKGROUND

Patmos, from which John wrote, and where he was exiled for "the word of God," was a small, rocky, desolate, unimportant island in the Aegean Sea. This crescent-shaped isle was approximately 24 miles from the western coast of Asia Minor and 72 miles southwest of Ephesus with an area of about 8 by 4 miles. Banishment to such an island was a common punishment in the Roman Empire, usually for the remainder of one's life. Whether John may have suffered further by being sentenced to hard labor is not entirely clear. At any rate, he wrote to the seven churches as a "brother" in their suffering.

Asia Minor is a 250,000 square mile peninsula surrounded by the Black, Aegean, and Mediterranean Seas. Also called Anatolia, it is the westernmost protrusion of Asia and comprises most of the Asian part of modern Turkey and the Armenian highland.

Each of the cities to whom the letters were addressed played a vital role in the life of Asia Minor. Each enjoyed either economic, spiritual, or political prominence in the region. Further, each was tied, in some way, to the Roman imperial cult.

Through the letters, John purports that Christ speaks through him by the Holy Spirit to the prevailing situation within the seven churches. Each received a spiritual checkup and a "report card." The living Christ assesses their strengths and weaknesses as well as their dangers and opportunities. In each case, He is aware of the true spiritual condition of each congregation since nothing is hidden from God's sight.

In his writing, John reveals specific symbolic attributes of Christ's character which he says were given to him in the vision. For him, Christ:

8

- Holds the seven stars in His right hand and walks in the midst of seven candlesticks

- Is the first and last, who was dead and is alive

- Has the sharp two-edged sword

- Has the seven spirits of God

- Has eyes like a flame of fire and feet like fine brass

- Is Holy and true; has the key of David; opens and no one can shut, shuts and no one can open

- Is the Amen, the faithful and true witness, the beginning of the creation of God

Taken together, these attributes reveal a picture of Christ as shining brilliantly and terrifyingly to His foes. This is a picture of an overpowering victor. These attributes further attempt to depict the full nature of God in dealing with the church throughout its history. They also relate symbolically to some attributes of the specific cities in which the churches were located.

The salutation in verses 4 and exhortation in 11 indicate that the entire book—not just the portion dealing with their respective situation—was written to the churches as a group. Verse 11 specifically commands the writer to write all he sees and send the entire scroll to all the churches. Our study, however, deals in detail with the particular messages directed specifically to each of them.

These are prophetic letters like we see in 2 Chronicles 21:12–15 and Jeremiah 29 and resemble ancient royal and imperial edicts, such as would have been written by the Roman rulers. They also closely resemble the biblical format of oracles concerning various peoples such as we see in Isaiah 13–23; Jeremiah 46–51; Ezekiel 25–32; and Amos 1–2.

EXPOSITION:

Each letter follows a specific pattern. Numeric symbolism is repeated throughout the entire book. Yet, the number seven is symbolic of completeness in apocalyptic literature. There are seven churches headed by seven angels. Christ has seven spirits of God, holds seven stars in his hands, and walks among seven lampstands.

The "angel" of each church is either the pastor of the congregation or real angels with designated responsibility for protecting the respective churches. In either case, they are the responsible subject to whom the letter is addressed, have oversight of each church and the ultimate obligation to ensure that the mandates of the letter are carried out.

This is not a personal vision to be closely held by the one who received it. It is to be shared, for he is explicitly told to write what he has seen. A special blessing is reserved for those who read it and act on what they have read.

The postal route, covering the seven cities, ran along the wide vale into the Hermos Valley. If the letters circulated in the order of the named churches, They would encompass a rough circle, another symbol of completeness. However, these seven churches, by no means, represent the church in the sense of what a Christian community should be. Rather, taken together, the entirety of what is good and evil in the church; its strengths and weaknesses, what is to be kept and nurtured, revitalized or discarded are laid out.

A further symbolic pattern is seen in the arrangement of the seven-fold message. Churches 1 and 7 are in grave danger, 2 and 6 are in excellent shape, and 3, 4, and 5 are neither particularly good nor extremely evil.

John constructs each of the seven letters using the same pattern: Each contains:

1. An address (naming the recipient church)
2. A characteristic image of the Christ (who addresses the church)
3. An examination of the church's current spiritual standing
   a. A commendation (introduced by the words "I know...")
   b. A condemnation ("but I have this against you...")
   c. A warning
4. An ending refrain
   a. An admonition to act
   b. An encouragement
   c. A promise to the overcomer ("to the one who overcomes...")
   d. A general admonition to hear ("...what the Spirit says to the Churches")

When one or more of these elements are missing, it is a key to understanding the special situation of that church. Themes are offered repeatedly to reinforce the urgency with which the writer is conveying the message. It is important not only that the churches hear it, but that they understand and act— decode the symbols and apply what is said in securing their safety from the forces which threaten them from within and from without.

One of each of the seven characteristics of Christ will be revisited in the separate letters. For each has some significance for the congregation to which it is attached.

In the end, it is Christ who addresses each church. He makes any assessment of its spiritual condition. He issues the commendation and/or condemnation. He gives the warning and admonition. But importantly, it is also Christ who, ultimately promises assurance, and brings comfort to those who suffer distress.

With all the drama of a Hollywood thriller, the writer of the book of Revelation has a front row seat to a spectacular exhibition. First, he hears a booming voice sounding like a trumpet's blast; which is startling enough. Then, he turns to see an alarming, larger than life figure that so frightened him that he became faint.

In the text, John paints a graphic portrait of the one who is Christ. As he describes Him,

- He was clothed with a garment down to the feet and girded around the chest with a golden band;
- His head and hair were white like wool, as white as snow;
- His eyes like a flame of fire;
- His feet were like fine brass, as if refined in a furnace; and
- His voice as the sound of many waters.

John was having a theophany —a visible manifestation, of the presence of God, like God's appearance to Old Testament personalities such as Abraham and Moses. Examples of other New Testament theophanies include Jesus appearance to the disciples, Peter, James, and John, on the Mount of Transfiguration and Paul's encounter with Jesus on the Damascus Road. The portrait the writer paints denotes the strength, wisdom, passion, sureness, and glory of the risen Christ.

Repeatedly Christ reassures the writer and the reader that his promised return is imminent as measured in eternal moments. "I come quickly," He says to a church that may have grown weary in waiting. Yet, he reassures them that "He *is* coming... and every eye"—both of those who have been faithful as well as of those who have not; those who are waiting patiently and those who are not—"will see Him."

PERSONAL APPLICATION: TEN QUESTIONS FOR DISCUSSION

1. What overall impression do you have of what the writer is saying to introduce his letters to the churches?

2. What attributes of Christ do the elements of the greeting in chapter 1 to the respective churches suggest? Explain.

Element	Scripture Reference	Attribute Suggested
Holds the seven stars in his right hand and walks in midst of seven candlesticks	1:13a, 16; 2:1	
The first and last, who was dead and is alive	1:11a, 16, 18a; 2:8	
Has the sharp two-edged sword	1:16; 3:1	
Has seven spirits of God and the seven stars	1:16; 2:12	
Has eyes like a flame of fire and feet like fine brass	1:14b-15a; 2:18	
Holy, true has the key of David; opens and no one can shut; shuts and no one can open	1:5; 3:7	
The Amen, the faithful and true witness, the beginning of the creation of God	1:5a; 3:14	

3. The letters were written to Christians facing strong persecution. Where and in what ways do you feel the church is facing persecution today?

4. Describe a situation in which you were persecuted for your faith or stand as a Christian. What was your response?

5. The writer uses two symbolic measures in his letters: The number seven and the circle. What do these indicate for this correspondence?

6. The writer says that he was "in the Spirit." What does that language convey?"

7 Describe and experience when you were "in the Spirit." What did you take away from the experience?

8. The writer also speaks of hearing the Lord's voice. Have you ever had such an occasion? Describe the experience.

9. What does it mean that Christ describes himself as, "the Alpha and the Omega, the First and the Last?"

10. John describes himself as "your brother and companion" in the tribulation and kingdom and patience of Jesus Christ. What comfort do you think this brought to those who received these letters?

DAILY DEVOTIONAL READING:

DAY 1 - Revelation 1

DAY 2 - Revelation 2

DAY 3 - Revelation 3

DAY 4 - Revelation 19

DAY 5 - Revelation 20

DAY 6 - Revelation 21:1-13

DAY 7 - Revelation 21:14-27

==

LESSON 2: EPHESUS - THE LOVELESS CHURCH
Revelation 2:1-7

1 "To the angel of the church of Ephesus write, 'These things says He who holds the seven stars in His right hand, who walks in the midst of the seven golden lampstands:

2 "I know your works, your labor, your patience, and that you cannot [c]bear those who are evil. And you have tested those who say they are apostles and are not, and have found them liars;

3 and you have persevered and have patience, and have labored for My name's sake and have not become weary.

4 Nevertheless I have this against you, that you have left your first love.

5 Remember therefore from where you have fallen; repent and do the first works, or else I will come to you quickly and remove your lampstand from its place—unless you repent.

6 But this you have, that you hate the deeds of the Nicolaitans, which I also hate.

7 "He who has an ear, let him hear what the Spirit says to the churches. To him who overcomes I will give to eat from the tree of life, which is in the midst of the Paradise of God."

BACKGROUND:

Ephesus, the largest, most important, and capital city of Asia Minor had a population of more than a quarter of a million people by the time the letter was written. It was the commercial, political and religious center of Proconsul Asia and one of the major cosmopolitan cities of the Roman world. Located three miles from the coast where the Cayster and Meander Rivers enter the Aegean Sea, much Eastern trade was done through its port. Its highways connected the interior of Asia with all her chief cities.

The emperor had made Ephesus a free city and it was given the title "Supreme Metropolis of Asia." It also contained one of the seven wonders of the ancient world, the temple of Diana, completed in 323 B.C.E. It was ., a center of mystical cult worship of Diana, or Artemis, the Roman fertility goddess. There were also temples to the Roman emperors, Claudius, Hadrian, and Severus.

The Ephesian church was the most prominent of the seven and was considered a mother of the Asian churches. It had been established by Paul on his third missionary journey. Though Paul's first visit to the city was brief, he labored in there longer than in any other place. He taught in the synagogue for three months, followed by two years of teaching in the school of Tyrannus. and his work was responsible for establishing one of the strongest, most effective, prestigious first century congregations. many were saved and the gospel was heard throughout Asia Minor.

Through the work of this congregation, many converts made a complete break with the magic of their pagan past and burned their books publicly, books that were worth 50,000 pieces of silver. As a result, the gospel continued to flourish in Ephesus.

The size and dedication of the Ephesian church became a threat to the idol-making industry in the city. Led by Demetrius, a silversmith, a trade guild violently opposed Paul and the Ephesian church. They formed an angry mob and seized two of Paul's companions. While some Ephesian political officials restrained Paul from going before the hostile mob, the town clerk persuaded the crowd to settle their dispute in the courts, not in the street.

Some of the greatest leaders in the early church served here. Timothy was its first bishop, Priscilla, Aquilla, and Apollos, among others, had the benefits of personal instruction from these leaders. John is said to have ministered here, and the city became his residence before and after his exile.

DESCRIPTION OF CHRIST:	He who holds the seven stars in his right hand and who walks in the midst of the seven lampstands.
COMMENDATION:	Your toil and patient endeavor, you cannot bear evil persons, you have tested them who call themselves Apostles and found them to be false.
CONDEMNATION:	You have abandoned your first love.
WARNING:	Unless you repent, I will remove your lampstand from its place.
ENCOURAGEMENT:	You have this one thing, you hate the Nicolaitans which I hate also.
ADMONITION:	Repent, do your first works. Remember from where you have fallen.
PROMISE TO THE OVERCOMER:	I will grant you to eat of the tree of life.

EXPOSITION:

"He who walks in the midst..." is one of the characteristics of Christ that was introduced int the first chapter and denotes God's intimate involvement with these churches.

We know more about the church at Ephesus than about any of the others. This was the same congregation commended by Paul in the Book of Ephesians for their "faith and love for all the saints." So to consider from where it had fallen required looking back on a vital history of service and spiritual vigor.

This church dutifully went about its commitments. It was doctrinally sound, orthodox in every area, and spiritually discerning. But it fell severely short in the most vital quality of the Christian faith—LOVE. As the Apostle Paul said, to fall short in this one area is to be ineffective as a Christian. They were doing all the right things, but for the wrong reason, and with the wrong attitude.

The writer calls on them to remember their former state and return to the place where their love for the things of God was intense. Moreover, they were warned that if they did not act quickly, God's judgment would come upon them swiftly. For this church, to whom much had been given—that should have set the example to the other churches—much was being required. This congregation had been entrusted with the ministry of some of the Church's most spiritually prominent leaders and, in turn, would have been expected to remain a strong congregation.

The thing in their favor was their hatred for the Nicolaitans. These were followers of Nicolas, one of the first of six men chosen with the martyred Stephen, and ordained to the diaconate by the Apostles. He later succumbed to the heresy of Gnosticism that swept away many in the early church. Members of the group led lives of unrestrained indulgence.

The promise of being able to eat from the tree of life is reminiscent of the opening scenes of Scripture, where we encountered that tree in the Garden of Eden. The symbolism here holds the ultimate promise of eternal life and the return to the state for which we were created

THE CHURCH IN HISTORY: The Apostolic Church (30-99)

The earliest history of Christianity starts with the ministry of Jesus (c. 27–29 C.E.)and runs until the death of the last of the Twelve Apostles (c. 100 C.E.). This period was, perhaps, the most unspoiled because early Christians received pure doctrine either from the mouth of Jesus or from those who were close to Him. Yet, during this time, the Church evolved from a small Jewish sect to embrace a Gentile culture that absorbed many religious, cultural, and intellectual traditions of the Greco-Roman world in which it existed.

Following Christ's resurrection, believers expected the immediate installment of the Kingdom of God. First century churches were known for their faith, love, zeal, giving, knowledge, and intolerance for sin, as they anticipated the glorious occasion.

But the century ended on a less than promising note. False teachers crept into the community and began to introduce their counterfeit doctrines. And, this once obscure group began to be noticed by the Roman authorities. With this notice, came the beginning of a prolonged period of persecution.

Two of the most notable features of this period within the Roman empire were emperor worship and the adoration of the various deities. Temples were built, meat sacrifices were offered, temple prostitutes seduced worshippers who often involved themselves in orgies in the name of religion.

In 62 CE, James was executed in Jerusalem by the Sanhedrin. A few years later, Paul was executed in Rome by Nero. By the century's end, each of the original Apostles, besides the letter's conveyor, had experienced an ignoble death, and he was living in exile.

PERSONAL APPLICATION: TEN QUESTIONS FOR DISCUSSION:

1. What is your overall impression of the Ephesian Church?

2. This church is commended for their toil and patient endeavor. What does this suggest to you? When are we as Christian called on to patiently work for Christ?

3. The church is also commended for not bearing evil persons. What does this suggest?

4. Finally, the church is commended for having tested those who call themselves Apostles and found them to be false. What are the signs that let us differentiate between a true and false Apostle?

5. What does it mean that this church has left its first love? How can we, as Christians, lose our first love?

6. How is it possible for the Ephesian church to have fallen so far, considering its glorious beginnings and early leadership?

7. How does one rekindle spiritual love?

8. In what ways is there a need for such a rekindling today? Explain your answer?

9. The admonition to the church is to repent! What does true repentance look like?

10. The promise to this church is "I will give to eat from the tree of life, which is in the midst of the Paradise of God." What does this suggest to you?

DAILY DEVOTIONAL READING:

DAY 1 – Acts 15; 20:25-32

DAY 2 - Ephesians 1

DAY 3 – Ephesians 2

DAY 4 - Ephesians 3

DAY 5 - Ephesians 4

DAY 6 - Ephesians 5

DAY 7 - Ephesians 6

LESSON 3: SMYRNA - THE SUFFERING CHURCH
(Revelation 2:8-11)

⁸ "And to the angel of the church in Smyrna write,

'These things says the First and the Last, who was dead, and came to life:

⁹ "I know your works, tribulation, and poverty (but you are rich); and I know the blasphemy of those who say they are Jews and are not, but are a synagogue of Satan.

¹⁰ Do not fear any of those things which you are about to suffer. Indeed, the devil is about to throw some of you into prison, that you may be tested, and you will have tribulation ten days. Be faithful until death, and I will give you the crown of life.

¹¹ "He who has an ear, let him hear what the Spirit says to the churches. He who overcomes shall not be hurt by the second death."

BACKGROUND:

Smyrna was a seaport city about 35 miles north of Ephesus. It has been described as the most beautiful of the seven cities. Smyrna sat at the head of the gulf into which the Hermos river disperses. It was situated on a well-protected harbor at the natural terminus of a major inland trade route up the Hermos Valley, surrounded by rich farmland. Today it is called Izmir, Turkey

It was famous in its day for science, medicine, and majestic buildings. The name Smyrna may also have been taken from the ancient Greek word for myrrh, which was the chief export of the city in ancient times.

The second Asian temple to the Roman Emperor, Tiberius was built there after 26 B.C.E. Also a Caesar cult existed there.

Founded as a Greek colony one thousand years before Christ had been destroyed by an earthquake and rebuilt several times the city; each time more beautiful than the previous. But, destroyed by the Lydians in the 7th Century B.C.E., it was only a shell of its past glory for approximately 400 years, and then was rebuilt. From the time of this rebuilding, it was a faithful ally of Rome; and under the Roman government, it enjoyed prosperity and peace.

 Scripture does not give us any information concerning the founding of this church.

DESCRIPTION OF CHRIST:	The first and the last, he who was dead and is alive.
COMMENDATION:	Your affliction and poverty-yet you are rich. You have borne the slander of those who say they are Jews and are not, but are of the household of Satan.
CONDEMNATION:	No condemnation was given.
WARNING:	No warning is given.
ENCOURAGEMENT:	Do not fear the tribulation, you will suffer; be strong and faithful unto death.
ADMONITION:	The devil will put some in prison to test you, you will suffer persecution for ten days.
PROMISE TO THE OVERCOMER:	I will give you a crown of life. You will not be hurt by the second death.

EXPOSITION:

In the middle of persecution, the church at Smyrna was given a comforting word. The tone of this portion of the letter is affectionate and approving. The language "was dead and is alive" was a striking analogy to the early history of the city's — repeated destruction and rebuilding — which that local church would easily recognize. The depiction of Christ as "he who was dead and is alive" can be contrasted with the strong rebuke later given to the church at Sardis as having a name of being alive but was dead.

Some false prophets in the congregation (who said they were Jews, but were really of the household of Satan) were causing problems in the congregation. John's reference has been interpreted in two ways. One is that these were Gentiles who called themselves "Jews," but instead of following Judaism, worshiped the Roman emperor and spoke against the Christians in Smyrna. The other is that these were actually Jews who followed tradition and the Mosaic Law. They did not have the faith of their father Abraham, who looked forward to the promise of God, and had rejected Jesus Christ as their Messiah. Either way, they were instrumental in persecuting the church. John sees their impetus as coming from "Satan."

His words are not an indictment of all Jews, though such faulty interpretation has contributed to much anti-Semitism. The writer shows the same contempt for those Jews who come against the faith community in Smyrna that he evidenced for those non-Jews in Ephesus who falsely represented themselves as Apostles. His concern is not a license to denigrate Jews or any other ethnic group. For John, who was Jewish himself, the problem was those who persecute the church, no matter what their ethnic, social, or political persuasion.

The Smyrnean Church was commended for being hardworking and bearing tribulation, and material poverty, while being spiritually rich. The stark contradiction came from the fact that though located among the wealth of a very prosperous city, the church itself was materially poor.

The members of this congregation are encouraged to not be afraid of the tribulation they will surely encounter. Further, he entreats them to remain strong and faithful even in the face of death. The writer is very direct that some members of this congregation will be imprisoned as a test of their faith. Though the persecution was to be particularly harsh, this period could be measured. Though the number, "ten" days, is only figurative, he assured them their persecution will only last for a season. It would come to an end and the church would live through and survive it.

The "crown of life" was a play on the "Crown of Smyrna;" a referral to the skyline formed by the city's stately buildings that encircled the rounded sides of the hill of Pagos. The crown was also reminiscent of the garland of flowers worn at public ceremonies of faithful Roman citizens. Public servants who had served laudably were honored by having their likeness depicted on Smyrnean coins with laurel wreaths on their heads.

Since physical death was a real possibility for these Christians, the promise of escape from the "second death" held real hope. This is an affirmation that though they may have been facing physical death, in the end, they would live eternally.

THE CHURCH IN HISTORY- The Persecuted Church (100-313)

During the 2nd century, the Apostolic Fathers began to develop the teaching that would be foundational for Christian doctrine going forward.

While the Jewish Christian church was still centered in Jerusalem, Gentile Christianity began to blossom. Although the use of the term Christian is seen in the Acts of the Apostles (80–90 C.E.), the earliest recorded use of the term Christianity outside of Scripture is by Ignatius of Antioch, about 107 C.E.

Practically all Roman emperors during the 2nd and 3rd centuries persecuted Christians, but ten of these were more pronounced than the rest. In the second century, the major persecution was confined to Rome. They were under Nero, Domitian (under whom John suffered and was banished to Patmos), Trajan and Hadrian.

In the third century, though Roman persecution continued under Severus and Maximinus, empire-wide persecution of Christians began under the reign of Decius. This continued under Falerian and Aurelian. And according to historical accounts, the last and most bloody persecution took place under Diocletian and lasted 10 years.

Under the direction of these Roman leaders, thousands of faithful believers suffered harsh persecution including death. Martyrdom, including being crucified, fed to animals or forced to fight professional gladiators or burned at the stake, was common. Those who did not lose their lives, lost their livelihood or their standing in the community. In other words, they became poor for Christ's sake.

The extent of Smyrnan persecution can be understood by the fact that Polycarp, Bishop of the city, was martyred there. And according to some early writers, the city's unbelieving Jews joined with the Gentiles in condemning him to death and were so zealous that they ran to get fuel" for the fire.

It was during this period that some of the major heresies of the faith began to take root. Some major figures declared to be heretics were Marcion, Valentinus, and Montanus.

PERSONAL APPLICATION - TEN QUESTIONS FOR DISCUSSION

1. What is your overall impression of the Church at Smyrna?

2. This is a church that received no condemnation and no warning. What does this say to you?

3. Do you feel that there is any segment of the church today that can enjoy the distinction of deserving no condemnation and no warning from God? Talk about this.

4. What does it mean to you that the writer describes this church as rich in the midst of poverty? What does a spiritually rich church look like?

5. What does a spiritually rich individual look like?

6. One form of persecution borne by this congregation was the slander of those who say they are Jews but are of the household of Satan. Have you ever been slandered for your faith? What should be our reaction to such a test?

7. What hope does the writer provide us when we as individual Christians or as the church are facing persecution?

8. Look for other passages in scripture that deal with the persecution of Christians. What insight do they provide regarding how we should view or deal with persecution?

9. Though most of us are not called on to die, literally, for our faith, in many parts of the globe, martyrdom, imprisonment, or social isolation is a reality. What encouragement can we offer these Christians?

10. What encouragement does the promise that the overcomer will receive "a crown of life" and "will not be hurt by the second death" bring to us.?

DAILY DEVOTIONAL READING:

DAY 1 - Luke 12:1-13

DAY 2 - I Peter 1-2

DAY 3 - I Peter 3

DAY 4 - I Peter 4

DAY 5 - James 1

DAY 6 - John 1:46-48

DAY 7 - Psalm 32

===

LESSON 4: PERGAMOS - THE HERETICAL CHURCH
Revelation 2:12-17

12 "And to the angel of the church in Pergamos write, 'These things says He who has the sharp two-edged sword:

13 "I know your works, and where you dwell, where Satan's throne is. And you hold fast to My name, and did not deny My faith even in the days in which Antipas was My faithful martyr, who was killed among you, where Satan dwells.

14 But I have a few things against you, because you have there those who hold the doctrine of Balaam, who taught Balak to put a stumbling block before the children of Israel, to eat things sacrificed to idols, and to commit sexual immorality.

15 Thus you also have those who hold the doctrine of the Nicolaitans, which thing I hate.

16 Repent, or else I will come to you quickly and will fight against them with the sword of My mouth.

17 "He who has an ear, let him hear what the Spirit says to the churches. To him who overcomes I will give some of the hidden manna to eat. And I will give him a white stone, and on the stone a new name written which no one knows except him who receives it.

BACKGROUND:

Pergamos was located approximately 60 miles north of Smyrna and 15 miles from the Aegean Sea. The official capital of Asia Minor, it was the chief city of the Province of Mysia, in the Caisus Valley.

The city was the center of four pagan cults: Zeus, Athena, Dionysus, and Aesclepius, whose symbol was the serpent. It was one of the most prominent centers of the imperial cult and the seat of Emperor worship. The first temple to the worship of the Roman emperor Caesar as a divine being. was erected in 29 B.C.E. The shrine to Aesclepius held a spa used for natural and supernatural healing rites.

The city was an ancient seat of culture, whose 20,000-volume library rivaled that of the great libraries in Alexandria. It was here that parchment was invented so that paper could be used for the transcribing of books for its library.

DESCRIPTION OF CHRIST:	He who has the sharp two edge sword.
COMMENDATION:	You hold fast my name and have not denied my faith even in the face of martyrdom; in the place where Satan dwells.
CONDEMNATION:	You have some who hold to the teaching of Balaam and some who hold to the teaching of the Nicolaitans.
WARNING:	I will come quickly and will fight against them with the sword of my mouth.
ENCOURAGEMENT:	No encouragement was given.
ADMONITION:	Repent.
PROMISE TO THE OVERCOMER:	Some of the hidden manna and a white stone with a new name written on it that no one knows.

EXPOSITION:

Pergamos (variously referred to as Pergamon or Pergamum) was a city dedicated to the worship of many gods, and to declare oneself a Christian who only worshipped the "one true God and Savior Jesus Christ" would certainly have provoked hostility. How much easier it would have been to simply keep one's faith and convictions private and do what one had to do to get by.

The church at Pergamos was a church of divided loyalties. It had withstood the external threat of martyrdom, but had become vulnerable to the internal danger of heresy.

Those who followed Balaam in the book of Numbers used Midianite women to seduce the men of Israel and lead them to worship other gods. The New Testament tells us that his followers forsook the right way, and went astray because Balaam "loved the wages of unrighteousness."

On the other hand, the teaching of the same Nicolaitans, which was hated by the Ephesian church, was embraced by some members of this church. Though we do not know exactly what this teaching was, we know it was related to Gnosticism

In the letter, the writer designates the city as "the place where Satan dwells" and reiterates that it is the place of "Satan's throne." This can be interpreted as the center of imperial cult worship of the emperor. Or it can be viewed as the seat of the Roman government where the governor had once lived at the time of the writing and where he regularly held court. At any rate, it denotes a particularly wicked place, a difficult and hostile place for the church to exist, and suggest that it took a high degree of spiritual fortitude and warfare to exist in Pergamos.

This warfare is further indicated in the imagery of the sword. On a practical level, the two-edge sword contrasts, explicitly, with the sword of the governor since the Roman proconsul of Pergamos was vested with "the power of the sword." On a spiritual level, it indicates that though this church would be engaged in battle, it would, ultimately, be God who would be fighting for them.

Christ makes three promises to overcomers in Pergamos. They will receive hidden manna, a white stone, and a new name. Jewish believers in Christ were aware of the tradition that held that before the destruction of the temple, Jeremiah hid the Ark of the covenant with the memorial manna in it from Israel's wilderness sojourn. This reference is a reminder of this cherished memory for the faith community. Yet as earlier, as that manna physically sustained the Israelites through their desert wanderings, those at Pergamos would be strengthened and sustained spiritually.

The white stones have variably been interpreted as a medium for the recording names, a signifier a judge puts into a vessel to vote a person's acquittal, or as an admission ticket to a feast or celebration. The promise of a new name, which no one but the one who receives it indicates both the intimacy with which God knows each of us and the private invitation for our presence at God's banquet table.

THE CHURCH IN HISTORY- Early Medieval Church (313-537)

During this period, the church began to gain some prominence under Constantine. After his conversion, he became a patron of the Church, giving it imposing and lavishly decorated Basilicas as well as extravagant gifts of money. He also supplied the clergy with superb vestments and clad Bishops in costly robes and seated them on a lofty throne in the apse of the Basilica, with a marble altar, adorned with gold and gems, on a lower level in front of him.

Under his direction, the church married the world. Heathen priests became Christian priests and heathen temples became Christian churches. All children were required to be christened, supposedly, making them Christian. Heathen days of feasting and drunkenness were made into Christian observances and various saints' days. For illustration, December 25th was regarded throughout the Roman world as the "birthday" of the "Sun God" and a high festival celebrated by the "Great Games" of the Circus. So the birthday of Jesus was changed from April, when he was probably born, to that date.

Because of Constantine's intervention, the Church was becoming rich and powerful. It was thought that uniting Church and State would set up a condition that would usher in the Millennium. And, in essence, Christianity became a mass state religion. Since scriptural support was needed for such a doctrine, it was claimed that the Jews had been cast off, and the prophecies of Israel's future glory were intended for the Church.

PERSONAL APPLICATION - TEN QUESTIONS FOR DISCUSSION

1. What is your overall impression of the Church at Pergamos?

2. What does the imagery of Christ as "He who has the sharp two-edged sword" suggest?

3. How would you define heresy?

4. How do we discern between true heresy and a simple difference of opinion on matters of faith?

5. To what heresies is the contemporary church subject?

6. What is the story of Balaam? (See devotional readings). What import does it have for the writer's message to the church at Pergamos?

7. Make a case for the Nicolaitan's position regarding religious freedom.

8. A problem with this church was the temptation to compromise the truth of pure doctrine. What can we do to protect ourselves from this temptation?

9. The writer has only one word of admonition for this church: "Repent." Why is repentance so important for true change?

10. What do you take away from the promise of "hidden manna" and a "white stone with a new name written on it that no one knows except him who receives it?"

DAILY DEVOTIONAL READING:

DAY 1 - Numbers 22

DAY 2 - Numbers 23

DAY 3 - Numbers 24

DAY 4 - Numbers 31

DAY 5 - I Corinthians 8

DAY 6 - I Timothy 6

DAY 7 - I Peter 2:4-10

==

LESSON 5: THYATIRA - THE COMPROMISING CHURCH
Revelation 2:18-29

18 "And to the angel of the church in Thyatira write,

'These things says the Son of God, who has eyes like a flame of fire, and His feet like fine brass:

19 "I know your works, love, service, faith, and your patience; and as for your works, the last are more than the first.

20 Nevertheless I have a few things against you, because you allow that woman Jezebel, who calls herself a prophetess, to teach and seduce My servants to commit sexual immorality and eat things sacrificed to idols.

21 And I gave her time to repent of her sexual immorality, and she did not repent.

22 Indeed I will cast her into a sickbed, and those who commit adultery with her into great tribulation, unless they repent of their deeds.

23 I will kill her children with death, and all the churches shall know that I am He who searches the minds and hearts. And I will give to each one of you according to your works.

24 "Now to you I say, and to the rest in Thyatira, as many as do not have this doctrine, who have not known the depths of Satan, as they say, I will put on you no other burden.

25 But hold fast what you have till I come.

26 And he who overcomes, and keeps My works until the end, to him I will give power over the nations—

27 'He shall rule them with a rod of iron;

They shall be dashed to pieces like the potter's vessels — as I also have received from My Father;

28 and I will give him the morning star.

29 "He who has an ear, let him hear what the Spirit says to the churches

BACKGROUND:

Thyatira was an inland city on the boundary of Lydia and Mysia in what is present day Akhisar, Turkey. Situated in the long vale connecting the Hermos and Caicus valleys, the city was bounded by a major regional communications and trade route. It was probably the least important of the seven cities, although still a commercial center. Lydia, the seller of purple, and an avid supporter of the Apostle Paul was from Thyatira and had possibly been a member of this congregation.

Founded as a garrison city by Seleucus I, King of Pergamos, in the third century B.C.E., little is known of its history except that it changed hands as the fate of Pergamos changed.

Thyatira began to prosper under Roman rule. It was noted for its trade guilds that held an honored place in society. Fabric workers, garment makers and dealers, leather workers, tanners, potters, bakers, bronze-smiths, and slave dealers all had guilds in Thyatira. Membership was considered necessary for furthering business success and having access to the amenities necessary for a "good life."

There is circumstantial evidence that Paul may have visited this city and church during his third missionary journey.

DESCRIPTION OF CHRIST:	He who has eyes like a flame of fire and feet like fine and searches the regions and hearts.
COMMENDATION:	Your works, love, faith, service, endurance; your latter works greater than the first.
CONDEMNATION:	You tolerate that woman Jezebel, who calls herself a prophetess, teaches and beguiles my servants to practice immorality and eat food sacrificed to idols.
WARNING:	I will throw her on a sickbed and those who commit adultery with her into great tribulation, unless they repent; and will strike her children dead.
ENCOURAGEMENT:	On those who do not hold to the teachings of Jezebel I lay no other burden.
ADMONITION:	Repent (to those who follow the teachings of Jezebel). Hold fast to what you have until I come (to the entire church). I will give to everyone according to their works.
PROMISE TO THE OVERCOMER:	You will have power over the nations, ruling them with a rod of iron and smashing them in pieces like earthen pots. I will give you the morning star.

EXPOSITION

Thyatira received the longest portion of the entire letters, although it was the smallest and least significant of the cities. Its letter begins with a strong affirmation. There is much to commend in this church. Characterized by love, faithfulness, service, and endurance, it showed evidence of growing in the fruit of the Spirit and maturing in Christian virtue. Like Pergamos, however, the church at Thyatira was divided. Yet, the Spirit distinguishes between these groups and does not offer blanket condemnation for the sins of a few.

There is a severe flaw in the spiritual character of the Thyatira n church. Perhaps, in an attempt to be loving and patient, the church allowed certain detestable behavior to go unchecked. It had allowed into fellowship a person who had openly challenged sound doctrine and ethical Christian conduct. She had been permitted to operate as a prophetess, teaching that sexual impurity was not a breach of Christian morality and that it was alright to eat meat that, knowingly, had been sacrificed to idols. More importantly, her teachings were causing some other members of the congregation to fall into sin.

Moreover, when confronted with her error, she refused to repent; yet she, still, was allowed to remain as a leader within the congregation. Indeed, she was probably belligerent about her right to teach whatever doctrine she saw fit.

Another problem for the Christians at Thyatira was the guilds to which some belonged. As an integral part of their proceeding, these guilds were deeply rooted in worshipping other gods. Further, their periodic banquets were often tainted with outbursts of drunkenness and sexual license.

The letter is clear. Jezebel, her children, and those who bought into her heretical and dangerous teaching, and practiced the ungodly behavior it promoted were subject to God's judgment. But because God is just, those who maintained purity of heart and action would be spared.

God reminds the congregation that He searches the mind and heart, the inner thoughts, of the individual, and rewards us accordingly. "Man looks on the outward appearance, but God looks at the heart" and sees us for who we truly are.

The promise to the overcomers in this congregation is that He will give himself to them. They will receive all of his life, all of his righteousness, all of his authority, all of his holiness, all of Him. They will be among the saints who will judge the world.

THE CHURCH IN HISTORY-Late Medieval Period (600-1517)

The late Middle Ages began with the first pope in the sixth century. The date 538 is suggested as its beginning date for when the decree issued by Byzantine Emperor, Justinian, uniting church and state went into effect.

Religious practice in this period was dominated by the Catholic Church. It was the single most powerful institution in medieval life, and its power was elevated to that of a king. The majority of the population was Christian, which at this time meant "Catholic"

By this period, the Church had an established hierarchy with the Pope as the head, Cardinals as advisors to the Pope and administrators of the Church, Bishops/Archbishops as ecclesiastical superiors over a cathedral or region, priests overseeing the local congregation.

But, the church was embroiled in compromise. It had begun to form economic and political alliances to ensure that it remained in power. Faithfulness to church ritual and doctrine replaced personal faith in Jesus Christ. The Bible was unavailable to ordinary Christians with tradition exalted in its place and works coming to be considered a means of gaining salvation.

At the same time, a series of famines and plagues, beginning with the Great Famine of 1315–1317 and including the Black Death (beginning 1347), decimated the European population. It is estimated that these conditions reduced the population by half or more.

Popular revolts, civil wars between nobles, and international conflicts between kings shattered the Catholic Church and its surrounding society. In the aftermath as a precursor to the

Reformation, the uncertainty that ensued saw people becoming dissatisfied with church structure and seeking a simpler, yet more vital faith

PERSONAL APPLICATION - TEN QUESTIONS FOR DISCUSSION

1. What is your overall impression of the Thyatira n Church?

2. How are the qualities of love, faith, service, and perseverance related?

3. What does the description of Christ as the "Son of God" imply, and why do you think it appears in this letter?

4. Who was Jezebel in the Old Testament? How does her story figure into the symbolism of the letter of this church?

5. Contrast the teachings of Jezebel and the Nicolaitans with those of Paul in Corinthians concerning eating meat sacrificed to idols. How are they different? Why do you suppose this is so?

6. Jezebel refused to repent when confronted with her sin. What are the consequences of an unrepentant heart?

7. In what situation in your life is it comforting to know that God sees and knows our mind and heart and will reward us according to our works? In which does it bring anxiety?

8. In each generation, Christians are challenged to function in society without participating in questionable practices when there are consequences for livelihood or social standing? What solution do you suggest?

9. How far should I go in accepting and adopting contemporary standards of moral conduct?

10. What false teachings tempt today's Christians?

DAILY DEVOTIONAL READING:

DAY 1 - I Kings 16

DAY 2 - I Kings 19

DAY 3 - II Kings 9

DAY 4 - Acts 16

DAY 5 - II Peter 1

DAY 6 - II Peter 2

Day 7 – Psalm 139

===

LESSON 6: SARDIS - THE LIFELESS CHURCH
Revelation 3:1-6

And to the angel of the church in Sardis write,

'These things says He who has the seven Spirits of God and the seven stars: "I know your works, that you have a name that you are alive, but you are dead.

2 Be watchful, and strengthen the things which remain, that are ready to die, for I have not found your works perfect before God.

3 Remember therefore how you have received and heard; hold fast and repent. Therefore if you will not watch, I will come upon you as a thief, and you will not know what hour I will come upon you.

4 You have a few names even in Sardis who have not defiled their garments; and they shall walk with Me in white, for they are worthy.

5 He who overcomes shall be clothed in white garments, and I will not blot out his name from the Book of Life; but I will confess his name before My Father and before His angels.

6 "He who has an ear, let him hear what the Spirit says to the churches

BACKGROUND:

The city of Sardis was located in western Asia Minor about fifty miles east of Smyrna and thirty miles southeast of Thyatira. The chief and, one-time, capital of the Province of Lydia was an important and wealthy metropolis located on the commercial trade route running east and west through the province. Sardis was founded in the 3rd Century B.C.E. It had been one of the richest and most powerful cities of the ancient world.

Sardis was famous for arts and crafts, and the first center to mint gold and silver coins. Within its limits could be found extensive fruit orchards, a large textile industry, and numerous jewelry factories. Much of its wealth, therefore, came from its textile manufacturing and dye industry and its jewelry trade. But, it had been ravaged both by fire and earthquakes, was at the time of the writing only a tiny, though still wealthy, village.

The city was situated on a mountain, surrounded by cliffs so steep that were almost impossible to scale and had only one narrow way of approach. It had, at one time, been considered to be impregnable because of its ideal physical arrangement and topography for defense. However, on two separate occasions, this fortified, presumably impenetrable, city had been attacked by surprise and conquered. This ancient city with a long history had come back into prominence under Roman rule.

During the period, the letter was written, the city was the center of the imperial cult of the region. It was devoted to the worship of the mother-goddess, Cybele, and no worshipper was allowed to approach the temple of the gods with soiled or unclean garments. A white, clean robe was required. Yet, worship of the goddess was of the most debasing nature, and orgies like those of Dionysus were practiced at the festivals held in her honor.

Most of the city took part in this pagan worship, and there were many mystery cults or secret religious societies. The magnificent Temple of Artemis dating from the fourth century B.C. was one of its points of interest and still exists as an important ruin. The remains of a Christian church building, which have been discovered immediately adjacent to the temple, testify of post-apostolic Christian witness to this wicked and pagan city noted for its loose living. The church to which the letter was addressed continued its existence until the fourteenth century, but it never was prominent. Today only a small village known as Sart exists amid the ancient ruins.

DESCRIPTION OF CHRIST:	He who has the seven spirits of God and the seven stars
COMMENDATION:	No commendation is given.
CONDEMNATION:	You have a name of being alive but are dead
WARNING:	If you do not awake, I will come as a thief and no one will know the hour.
ENCOURAGEMENT:	There are a few who have not defiled themselves who will walk with me in white.
ADMONITION:	Awake, strengthen that which remains. Remember what you have received and heard. Repent!
PROMISE TO THE OVERCOMER:	You will walk with Christ in white. I will not blot your name out of the book of life. I will confess your name before my father and His angels.

EXPOSITION:

Sardis is the first church in the letters in which there was nothing found to commend; a sad commentary, indeed, on its spiritual condition. This is especially true since it along with Thyatira, was one of the only two cities within the seven whose letter indicated no evidence of present or imminent persecution. The situation with the Christians at Sardis was one of relative ease, and within this comfortable situation, it had lulled itself to sleep.

No indication is given as to what the specific infraction was. There was no particular sin that was offensive such as the false teaching, idolatry, or sexual immorality of other congregations. There appears, rather, a general lack of spiritual vitality and a sense of lethargy throughout the whole congregation.

The church at Sardis was marked by complacency and had no inkling of its real spiritual situation. From the outside, this church was seen as thriving and, indeed, had proclaimed itself to be alive. It had a reputation of being filled with activity, action, and programs. By human standards, it was successful and was proud of the characterization. But the spirit's assessment was not that it was a dying church—in fact, it was dead! This is a harsh assessment.

Unlike Thyatira and Pergamos, where a minority had been involved in the immorality, all but a few in this church are incriminated. But there was a remnant who had not implicated themselves. And those few are admonished to remember what they had received from Christ and revive the little bit of life that remained.

The encouragement and promises to those who overcome are that they will walk with Christ in white, that their name will not be blotted out, and He will confess their name before the Father and His angels. The white garments are unsoiled by the Christians who were constantly threatened with being labeled as nonconformists and stripped of their Roman citizenship for refusing to denounce their faith. So here, the Lord personally promises the overcomer the safety of his heavenly citizenship. Further, the overcomer will experience a special reward in the form of public recognition.

THE CHURCH IN HISTORY – The Reformation Church (1517-1648)

The Reformation period began at a time when the Church was starting to reap the effects of centuries of compromise. It had grown large and powerful. Its increasing influence and wealth contributed to bankrupting the church as a spiritual force. Abuses such as the sale of indulgences (spiritual privileges) by the clergy, nepotism, and other evidence of corruption undermined the church's spiritual authority. The Mass was in Latin and though people were compelled to attend, they understood little that was said. And individuals, who were not clergy were still forbidden from reading Scripture.

The Reformation changed all that. During the relatively brief period of the next 100 years. From the one Catholic Church that dominated all of Christian life and practice as well as the religious, political, intellectual, and cultural affairs of the known Western world, several new denominations were born. The Lutherans, Calvinists (Presbyterian) Episcopalian, Methodist, and Baptist churches all got their start during this time.

These leaders originally had no intention of leaving the church. They called upon it to repent. The attempt to bring change was successful, but to untangle the web of corruption involved heavy inner church fighting, persecution of each other by the various factions and war.

But the acts of courageous reformers and the invention of the printing press freed Scripture from the Church's captivity and allowed it to be translated into the languages of the people. Because of this, individual believers were finally able to read the Bible for themselves and attempt to understand its message. The key ideas of the Reformation were a call to purify the church and a belief that the Bible, not tradition, and personal faith rather than an intermediary institution should be the sole source of spiritual authority for the believer.

PERSONAL APPLICATION - TEN QUESTIONS FOR DISCUSSION

1. What is your overall impression of the Church at Sardis?

2. What does the imagery of Christ as "He who has the seven Spirits of God and the seven stars" suggest?

3. Contrast and compare the signs of a lifeless church with that of a vital church?

4. How is it possible for a church to have a "good" reputation and yet be "dead"? How do you suppose a church could be spiritually dead and be completely unaware of it?

5. The writer exhorts the few faithful to "strengthen the things that remain." What "things" would be vital to the life of a church to prevent it from dying?

6. The writer also exhorts them to remember what they had received and heard. What does this suggest about the place of remembering in maintaining Christian vitality?

7. What steps do you think are important for a church to strengthen those things and ensure that it maintains its spiritual vitality?

8. The Sardis congregation had it relatively easy. Is persecution necessary for a church to maintain spiritual vitality?

9. The commendation for the church was that there were a few faithful ones who had not "soiled their garments." How would these words encourage those faithful to the Lord when all around them are unfaithful?

10. How does one remain strong in the faith when he/she is one among many who are compromising?

DAILY DEVOTIONAL READING:

DAY 1 - Ezekiel 37:1-14

Day 2 - Matthew 23:23-36

DAY 3 - Galatians 5

DAY 4 - Philippians 4

DAY 5 - I Thessalonians 5

DAY 6 - II Peter 3

DAY 7 - I John 2

===

LESSON 7: PHILADELPHIA - THE FAITHFUL CHURCH
Revelation 3:7-13

7 "And to the angel of the church in Philadelphia write,

'These things says He who is holy, He who is true, "He who has the key of David, He who opens and no one shuts, and shuts and no one opens":

8 "I know your works. See, I have set before you an open door, and no one can shut it; for you have a little strength, have kept My word, and have not denied My name.

9 Indeed I will make those of the synagogue of Satan, who say they are Jews and are not, but lie—indeed I will make them come and worship before your feet, and to know that I have loved you.

10 Because you have kept My command to persevere, I also will keep you from the hour of trial which shall come upon the whole world, to test those who dwell on the earth.

11 Behold, I am coming quickly! Hold fast what you have, that no one may take your crown.

12 He who overcomes, I will make him a pillar in the temple of My God, and he shall go out no more. I will write on him the name of My God and the name of the city of My God, the New Jerusalem, which comes down out of heaven from My God. And I will write on him My new name.

13 "He who has an ear, let him hear what the Spirit says to the churches

BACKGROUND:

Philadelphia was a Lydian city located beneath Mount Tomolus on a broad, low closely defended hillside in western Asia Minor. It was founded around 140 B.C.E. by the king of Pergamos, Attalus II Philadelphia, in honor of his brother. Destroyed by an earthquake in 17 C.E., for the next 20 years, it was tormented by recurring quakes. For some time after the earthquake, citizens sought temporary shelter in the surrounding countryside or left every evening, afraid to stay in their homes. The city was rebuilt with the help of Emperor, Tiberius. In gratitude, city leaders changed its name to Neoceasera (New Caesar). Sometime later, its name was changed again to Philadelphia Flavia.

It was a center of the worship of Dionysius, one of several deities whose popular adoration was practiced throughout the area. But the city contained temples to many other gods. The second Asian temple to Tiberius was built there after 26 B.E., and a Caesar cult existed there.

The city was called the gateway to central Asia Minor. It was famous for science, medicine, and majestic buildings. Its strategic location also made it a vital commercial link between Sardis and Pergamos on the west and Laodicea and Hierapolis on the east. Further, it was a prosperous agricultural center, situated in a vine growing and wine producing district, It was, as well, a heavy producer of leather and textiles.

DESCRIPTION OF CHRIST:	He that is holy, true, that has the key of David, that opens and no one can shut and that shuts and no one can open.
COMMENDATION:	You have but little power, yet you have kept my word and not denied my name
CONDEMNATION:	No condemnation is given.
WARNING:	No warning is given.
ENCOURAGEMENT:	I will make those of the Synagogue of Satan who say they are Jews but are not come and bow down at your feet and know that I love you.
ADMONITION:	Hold fast that which you have, that none can seize your crown.
PROMISE TO THE OVERCOMER:	You will become pillars in the Temple of my God and shall never go out of it. You will receive the name of my God and the name of the city of my God, and Christ's new name.

EXPOSITION

Only good was spoken of the Philadelphian church. No condemnation was levied against it and it received no warning. It obtained only commendation, encouragement, and promise, and appears to be a church over which the Spirit dotes.

This church was faithful in three areas. First, it kept Christ's word; second, it did not deny His name; third, it patiently endured its situation. It focused on faithfulness instead of fear amid trials and difficulties. And it was admonished to keep doing what it was doing so it would not lose the crown it had already attained. Because of this, it had the promise of Christ that, in the end, though they had endured harsh treatment, the congregation would not go through the same tribulation as the rest of the earth. Because they have proven to be faithful, God would keep them.

It is safe to assume that this was not a prestigious church—it had "little power," but was faithful. Christ appears to want to reward them with unlimited blessing—an open door which no one can shut! And no one can keep them from their reward. The nature of the impending persecution was not identified, but we can imagine that it would be severe since the church is encouraged to maintain its faithfulness in the face of death.

The writer speaks again of the synagogue of Satan and the Jews that were giving them some problems. This situation was similar to that in Smyrna. These Christians were being subjected to attack in the same way that those in their sister congregation, by slandering and blasphemy.

The promise to the overcomer is that they will be made a pillar in the temple of God, and shall go out no more. Further, they will have God's name and the name of the city of God—the New Jerusalem— Christ's new name written on them.

THE CHURCH IN HISTORY Modern Missionary Movement
(1648-1900)

In the centuries that followed the Reformation, the new churches had the power, resources, and felt the obligation to sending missionaries to evangelize most corners of the known world and spread the Christian message to many previously unreached people.

Many faithful Christians suffered hardship, persecution, and the loss of their lives as they attempted to bring the good news of the Gospel to those who had never heard it. They gave up careers and income, health or a comfortable standard of living to do what they felt called of God to do. And because of their efforts, there are very few areas of the globe that remain unreached by the Gospel.

Innovations in printing, communication, and transportation made it possible to translate the Scripture into various languages and disseminate it widely. Others undertook the painstaking, and often thankless, work of translating the Bible and making it available in every known language.

The later part of this period was also characterized by numerous revivalist movements that attempted to return the church to its earliest spiritual fervor and zeal—to make it alive again. Camp meetings, tent and healing revivals, and ever-new movements sought to recapture the enthusiasm and presence of God that was felt to be missing.

PERSONAL APPLICATION - TEN QUESTIONS FOR DISCUSSION:

1. What is your overall impression of the Church of Philadelphia?

2. What does the imagery of Christ as "He who is holy and true" suggest?

3. What does the imagery of Christ as "He who has the key of David" suggest?

4. What does the imagery of Christ as "He who opens and no one shuts, and shuts and no one opens" suggest?

5. What doors has God opened for you?

6. Why would having "a little power (strength)" be a positive and not a negative? What might He be implying here?

7. This is the second church that received no condemnation and no warning. How do you think it is possible to maintain such a state?

8. What are some circumstances in your life today in which you must persevere? How does this passage encourage you to press on?

9. What does it mean to us as believers that God will make unbelievers come and worship before our feet, and to know that God has loved us?

10. The promise to the overcomer is that, "I will make him a pillar in the temple of My God, and he shall go out no more." What does this suggest to you as a believer?

DAILY DEVOTIONAL READING:

DAY 1 - John 1:47-51

DAY 2 - Psalms 1

DAY 3 - I Thessalonians 4:13-18

DAY 4 - II Corinthians 12:1-10

DAY 5 - Matthew 5:1-12

DAY 6 - Luke 6:20-25

DAY 7 – John 14:16-27

==

LESSON 8: LAODICEA - THE LUKEWARM CHURCH
Revelation 3:14-21

14 "And to the angel of the church of the Laodiceans write,

'These things says the Amen, the Faithful and True Witness, the Beginning of the creation of God:

15 "I know your works, that you are neither cold nor hot. I could wish you were cold or hot.

16 So then, because you are lukewarm, and neither cold nor hot, I will vomit you out of My mouth.

17 Because you say, 'I am rich, have become wealthy, and have need of nothing'—and do not know that you are wretched, miserable, poor, blind, and naked—

18 I counsel you to buy from Me gold refined in the fire, that you may be rich; and white garments, that you may be clothed, that the shame of your nakedness may not be revealed; and anoint your eyes with eye salve, that you may see.

19 As many as I love, I rebuke and chasten. Therefore be zealous and repent.

20 Behold, I stand at the door and knock. If anyone hears My voice and opens the door, I will come in to him and dine with him, and he with Me.

21 To him who overcomes I will grant to sit with Me on My throne, as I also overcame and sat down with My Father on His throne.

BACKGROUND:

Laodicea was a wealthy city located in the Phygria region of the Lycus Valley in northwest Asia Minor. Its importance was due primarily to its position on the major east-west road between Ephesus and Syria.

The city's water supply was lukewarm, in contrast to the cold, pure waters of nearby Colossae or the famous hot springs at Hierapolis some five miles south. An aqueduct that probably carried water from the hot mineral springs of its neighbor would have become tepid before entering the city.

It was a prosperous, cosmopolitan, banking, and commercial city, with a large population of wealthy Jews. It was named for Laodice, wife of Antiochus II of Syria. A clothing manufacturing center, garments made there were world famous and Laodicean wool was a luxury commodity that dressed wealthy people of their time. Its renowned medical school was a center for callybrium, an eye salve.

According to Colossians 4:13-16, Laodicea, like Ephesus, received a personal correspondence from the Apostle Paul. Epaphras, one of his close companions from neighboring Colossae worked in this church and may have planted it. And, four times, Paul made mention of this congregation in his Colossian letter, which he instructed be shared with the sister church.

DESCRIPTION OF CHRIST:	The Amen, the witness on whom you can rely, and who is true, the cause of the creation of God.
COMMENDATION:	No commendation was given.
CONDEMNATION:	You are Lukewarm, neither hot nor cold. You say you are rich, prosperous and in need of nothing, but are wretched, poor, blind, and naked.
WARNING:	I will spew you out of my mouth."
ENCOURAGEMENT:	Those who I love, I reprove and chasten.
ADMONITION:	Buy from me gold refined by fire, white garments, eye salve.
PROMISE TO THE OVERCOMER:	If anyone opens the door I will come and sup with him and he with me. I will grant to sit with me in my throne.

EXPOSITION:

The fact that this is the only church to receive no commendation speaks volumes about its spiritual condition. There was nothing good that the Spirit had to say about, or to, this congregation.

To describe the church as "lukewarm" is not a compliment. The writer is accusing it of lacking enthusiasm or zeal "Neither hot nor cold," meant doing what they thought was just enough to get by spiritually.

Those who are "lukewarm" are actually in a worse condition than those who are "cold." They are not hot enough to be of use to the Kingdom, but they are not entirely indifferent to spiritual realities. Their surface, superficial interest makes their actions and attitude disgustingly distasteful to God. So much so that they leave a bitter taste in God's mouth.

The church is urged by the Spirit to buy things money cannot purchase: refined gold, white garments, and eye salve. These represent the major industries of Laodicea: banking, textiles, and medicine.

Gold refined by fire refers to intangible spiritual riches brought about by hard trials. This is costly faith that has been tested and is not perishable. In the end, such priceless faith brings lasting glory and honor to Christ.

In the ancient world, nakedness spoke of the worst kind of shame and humiliation, while to be finely clothed gave a sense of pride and designated honor and position. The stylishness, material wealth of the Laodiceans stands in stark contrast to the spiritual shame of the congregation. "White raiment"—spiritual clothing would cover this nakedness.

The church was also urged to buy eye salve to cure its spiritual blindness. It suffered from a deceptive sense of contentment and was unaware of its spiritual need because the accumulation of material goods and reliance on material wealth had blinded it to its true spiritual condition and lulled it into a false sense of security. Their motto may have been gain and more gain is godliness instead of the scriptural dictum that "godliness with contentment" is gain.

At first, the encouragement the church receives," those who I love, I reprove and chasten," hardly sounds heartening. Yet, any parent who genuinely loves their child and wants the best for them subjects them to discipline. This is no empty threat spoken in a moment of anger. Rather, it is for their own good that God will allow them to experience first the gentle voice of admonishment, and then the rod of correction. While the writer does not say what the chastening will be, the purpose of this reproof and chastening is to bring the church back to its former fervor. The end goal is repentance!

The promised to overcomers is that if they would take the first step and open the door, Christ will reward them royally. He will sit at the table and engage them in the intimate fellowship of the heavenly banquet. Their hunger and thirst for righteousness will be filled, and they will never experience emptiness again.

They will also sit with Him on His throne. As a queen sits beside her king and reigns with him from the throne room, so the overcoming Church—the Bride of Christ—will sit with Him, judging and reigning over the earth

THE CHURCH IN HISTORY Age of Apostacy (1900-present)

Scripture speaks of a time when, even among the people of God, everyone did what seemed right in their own eyes. Can it be that we find ourselves in such a time? On the surface, much is going on, but it can be largely mechanical with little God centered devotion. Committees, societies, and clubs are multiplied within the congregation and can take all our attention, but there can be an absence of "spiritual heat." Revival meetings are held, but instead of waiting on the Lord for power, they can become social events with soul winning and spiritual growth made a side business.

The contemporary church suffers from a spiritual sense of schizophrenia. It is outwardly rich by most standards. Yet, it suffers from a poverty of heart. Cathedral-like buildings, stained glass windows, eloquent preachers, richly paid musicians, and large, prosperous, and well-endowed congregations can be full of people, but spiritually empty.

Localities are saturated with large and small congregations of every denomination, and they can compete for prominence within a community. Yet, our neighborhoods, society, and world seem unaffected by our presence. And Church leaders appear afraid to address any issue that may threaten their economic or social standing.

Like the church at Laodicea, many in today's church are not burdened with debt, but with WEALTH. While we need the logistical resources money can buy, do we fail to understand that people are not converted by money, but by the Spirit of God working through passionate believers?

PERSONAL APPLICATION - TEN QUESTIONS FOR DISCUSSION:

1. What is your overall impression of the Laodicean Church?

2. What does the imagery of Christ as "the Amen, Faithful and True Witness, and Beginning of the creation of God" suggests?

3. What is the writer and the Spirit implying about this church by the term lukewarm?

4. What are the characteristics of a lukewarm church or Christian?

5. How do we keep ourselves or our church from getting to that state? What is the remedy for these types of problems according to this passage and how could such a remedy be practically applied?

6. Christ says that those whom He loves are subject to chastening. What does that look like? Can you relate to a time in your life when you were chastened by God? What did you learn?

7. Why do you think God would prefer that a church or an individual be either hot or cold, but not lukewarm?

8. Do you see any problems with the Laodicean church reflected in the contemporary church?

9. If we are truly dependent on God's faithfulness and truth, how does it impact the way we live our lives?

10. How can you "buy gold refined in the fire, white garments, and eye salve as the writer admonishes?

DAILY DEVOTIONAL READING:

DAY 1 - Isaiah 55

DAY 2- Ezekiel 16

DAY 3- Romans 12

DAY 4 - I Corinthians 3

DAY 5- I Timothy 6:1-6

DAY 6 - Hebrews 12:1-11

DAY 7 – Colossians 2; 4:12-17

LESSON 9: CONCLUSION
Revelation 21-:22

21 Then I saw a new heaven and a new earth; for the first heaven and the first earth passed away, and there is no longer any sea.

2 And I saw the holy city, new Jerusalem, coming down out of heaven from God, made ready as a bride adorned for her husband.

3 And I heard a loud voice from the throne, saying, "Behold, the tabernacle of God is among men, and He will dwell among them, and they shall be His people, and God Himself will be among them,

4 And He will wipe away every tear from their eyes; and there will no longer be any death; there will no longer be any mourning, or crying, or pain; the first things have passed away."

5 And He who sits on the throne said, "Behold, I am making all things new." And He *said, "Write, for these words are faithful and true."

6 Then He said to me, "It is done. I am the Alpha and the Omega, the beginning and the end. I will give to the one who thirsts from the spring of the water of life without cost.

7 He who overcomes will inherit these things, and I will be his God and he will be My son.

8 But for the cowardly and unbelieving and abominable and murderers and immoral persons and sorcerers and idolaters and all liars, their part will be in the lake that burns with fire and brimstone, which is the second death."

9 Then one of the seven angels who had the seven bowls full of the seven last plagues came and spoke with me, saying, "Come here, I will show you the bride, the wife of the Lamb."

10 And he carried me away in the Spirit to a great and high mountain, and showed me the holy city, Jerusalem, coming down out of heaven from God,

11 having the glory of God. Her brilliance was like a very costly stone, as a stone of crystal-clear jasper.

12 It had a great and high wall, with twelve gates, and at the gates twelve angels; and names were written on them, which are the names of the twelve tribes of the sons of Israel.

13 There were three gates on the east and three gates on the north and three gates on the south and three gates on the west.

14 And the wall of the city had twelve foundation stones, and on them were the twelve names of the twelve apostles of the Lamb.

15 The one who spoke with me had a gold measuring rod to measure the city, and its gates and its wall.

16 The city is laid out as a square, and its length is as great as the width; and he measured the city with the rod, fifteen hundred miles; its length and width and height are equal.

17 And he measured its wall, seventy-two yards, according to human measurements, which are also angelic measurements.

18 The material of the wall was jasper; and the city was pure gold, like clear glass.

19 The foundation stones of the city wall were adorned with every kind of precious stone. The first foundation stone was

jasper; the second, sapphire; the third, chalcedony; the fourth, emerald;

20 The fifth, sardonyx; the sixth, sardius; the seventh, chrysolite; the eighth, beryl; the ninth, topaz; the tenth, chrysoprase; the eleventh, jacinth; the twelfth, amethyst.

21 And the twelve gates were twelve pearls; each one of the gates was a single pearl. And the street of the city was pure gold, like transparent glass.

22 I saw no temple in it, for the Lord God the Almighty and the Lamb are its temple.

23 And the city has no need of the sun or of the moon to shine on it, for the glory of God has illumined it, and its lamp is the Lamb.

24 The nations will walk by its light, and the kings of the earth will bring their glory into it.

25 In the daytime (for there will be no night there) its gates will never be closed;

26 and they will bring the glory and the honor of the nations into it;

27 and nothing unclean, and no one who practices abomination and lying, shall ever come into it, but only those whose names are written in the Lamb's book of life.

22 Then he showed me a river of the water of life, clear as crystal, coming from the throne of God and of the Lamb,

2 in the middle of its street. On either side of the river was the tree of life, bearing twelve kinds of fruit, yielding its fruit every month; and the leaves of the tree were for the healing of the nations.

3 There will no longer be any curse; and the throne of God and of the Lamb will be in it, and His bond-servants will serve Him;

4 They will see His face, and His name will be on their foreheads.

5 And there will no longer be any night; and they will not have need of the light of a lamp nor the light of the sun, because the Lord God will illumine them; and they will reign forever and ever.

6 And he said to me, "These words are faithful and true"; and the Lord, the God of the spirits of the prophets, sent His angel to show to His bond-servants the things which must soon take place.

7 "And behold, I am coming quickly. Blessed is he who heeds the words of the prophecy of this book."

8 I, John, am the one who heard and saw these things. And when I heard and saw, I fell down to worship at the feet of the angel who showed me these things.

9 But he *said to me, "Do not do that. I am a fellow servant of yours and of your brethren the prophets and of those who heed the words of this book. Worship God."

10 And he *said to me, "Do not seal up the words of the prophecy of this book, for the time is near.

11 Let the one who does wrong, still do wrong; and the one who is filthy, still be filthy; and let the one who is righteous,

still practice righteousness; and the one who is holy, still keep himself holy."

12 "Behold, I am coming quickly, and My reward is with Me, to render to every man according to what he has done.

13 I am the Alpha and the Omega, the first and the last, the beginning and the end."

14 Blessed are those who wash their robes, so that they may have the right to the tree of life, and may enter by the gates into the city.

15 Outside are the dogs and the sorcerers and the immoral persons and the murderers and the idolaters, and everyone who loves and practices lying.

16 "I, Jesus, have sent My angel to testify to you these things for the churches. I am the root and the descendant of David, the bright morning star."

17 The Spirit and the bride say, "Come." And let the one who hears say, "Come." And let the one who is thirsty come; let the one who wishes take the water of life without cost.

18 I testify to everyone who hears the words of the prophecy of this book: if anyone adds to them, God will add to him the plagues which are written in this book;

19 and if anyone takes away from the words of the book of this prophecy, God will take away his part from the tree of life and from the holy city, which are written in this book.

20 He who testifies to these things says, "Yes, I am coming quickly." Amen. Come, Lord Jesus.

21 The grace of the Lord Jesus be with all. Amen.

BACKGROUND

At the end of his vision and the book, the writer reaffirms and expands God's promises to the faithful and challenges the paganistic worldview of his day. The whole of Revelation is meant to stir Christians' longing and prayers for the realization of God's purposes at the Second Coming and this is no more evident than at the end of the book.

The twelve foundation stones of the city wall are the twelve stones of the ancient zodiac. Pagans looked to the zodiac to guide their destiny because, supposedly, it reflects the order and purpose of life. Because John listed the twelve stones of the zodiac and, evidently, knew the meaning pagans attached to it. But John turned the tables on the pagan search for purpose and order, listing the stones in reverse order of their appearance in the zodiac and suggesting that the church, as the people of God, truly are in touch with the purpose and order of life. Throughout Revelation, martyrs and faithful saints experience victory. But the final victory, earlier anticipated in chapter 7, is being in the presence of God forever.

As early as the late first century, some Christians were moving away from a belief in the imminent return of Christ and settling in for the long haul. They were building institutions and adjusting to living alongside the Roman Empire. Centuries later, we still await the second coming of our Lord. But a fresh reading of this book's message reminds us that history will have its final resolution in the return of Christ. Until then, the writer calls the church to follow Christ rather than any political system, to be a holy people, and enjoy the promises reserved for faithful overcomers.

DESCRIPTION OF CHRIST:	He who sits on the throne. The root and the descendant of David. The bright morning star.
COMMENDATION:	Blessed is he who heeds the words of the prophecy of this book. Blessed are those who wash their robes, who have the right to the tree of life, and may enter by the gates into the city.
WARNING:	If anyone adds to words of the Book, God will add to him the plagues which are written in it. If anyone takes away from the words of the book of this prophecy, God will take away his part from the tree of life and from the holy city.
ENCOURAGEMENT:	God will wipe away every tear from their eyes. There will be no death, mourning, crying, pain, night, or curse. I am making all things new. I will give to the one who thirsts from the spring of the water of life without cost.

ADMONITION: Outside are the dogs, sorcerers, immoral persons, murderers, idolaters, and everyone who loves and practices lying.

Let the one who is righteous, still practice righteousness; and the one who is holy, still keep himself holy.

The part of the cowardly, unbelieving, abominable, murderers, immoral persons, sorcerers, idolaters, and liars will be in the lake that burns with fire and brimstone; the second death.

PROMISE: I am coming quickly.

EXPOSITION:

More than an end-time prophecy of doom or glory, the book of Revelation holds insight into the everyday and special struggles of Christian life in the early, as well as, contemporary Church. This study, then, calls upon Christians to hear and understand what the Spirit says to the church and wrestle with common issues that challenge faith in every age.

There is a progression. The church at Ephesus was characterized by loyalty to Christ but was lacking in love. In the church at Smyrna, loyalty was tested by fire. In the church at Pergamos, loyalties were divided. Yet none of the three churches had totally given in to the assaults of evil forces." In other words, they were still fighting.

With the church at Thyatira, as with those at Sardis and Laodicea, the situation was far more dangerous. Not merely a small minority were indifferent, but large numbers had yielded to the demoralizing influence of false doctrine and sinful behavior." There is a progressive worsening of the character of these churches as they become more and more influenced by evil until, finally, it takes over. Only the Philadelphian church has not succumbed

No more condemnation is given to the churches. However, they are strongly warned that anyone who adds to the words of not just the seven letters, but any part of the prophetic book, will be subject to the plagues which are written in it. Further, anyone who takes away from its words will have their part taken away from the tree of life and the holy city. This is severe counsel that should not be off-handedly dismissed.

Then the writer returns to the admonition that, outside are the dogs, sorcerers, immoral persons, murderers, idolaters, and everyone who lies whether in word or deed. He cautions us to be wary of entanglements that keep us for fully serving Christ.

The dogs—sorcerers, immoral persons, murderers, idolaters, and everyone who loves and practices lying is outside waiting to entangle the faithful in their web. Like wild mongrels, they desire to tear the believer away from the faith. And the caution is to stay away from them.

The admonition is for the one who is righteous to continue to be righteous; and the one who is holy to continue to be holy. This is a caution to keep away from those who are cowardly and unbelieving concerning faith, who commit vile, detestable, immoral or violent acts, those who practice witchcraft and the idolatry of false religion as well as those who are deceitful.

God considers all of this sin. And, in our contemporary culture of unbelief, this concluding admonition speaks of the reality of Hell—the lake that burns with fire and brimstone. This is the final home of those who refuse to repent of these detestable behaviors. And. it is here that they will partake in the second death—eternal separation from God.

The promise to all who overcome is that "I am coming quickly." For, in the end, though we suffer or are tempted to compromise, the church goes through spiritual vigor or decline, and the long wait for Christ's return seems unbearable, the ultimate triumph belongs to God. The supreme conqueror, promises to reward all those who faithfully stand with Christ and to make all things as they should be.

Tears, death, mourning, crying, pain, night, and all curses will be done away with. All things will be renewed, the one who experiences spiritual thirsts will be able to drink freely from the living water—Christ himself.

Even so, come quickly, Lord Jesus!

PERSONAL APPLICATION - TEN QUESTIONS FOR DISCUSSION:

1. Each letter instructs us to hear what the Spirit is saying to the church. What means does God use to speak to the church today?

2. What steps are important in ensuring that an individual or church can hear the Spirit speak? What things keep us from listening to or hearing the Spirit?

3. If Revelation 1-3 and 20-21 were written today, what would it say to the contemporary church at large?

4. What would it say to our denomination or congregation?

5. What would it say to us as individual Christians?

6. What do you take away from the warning regarding our relationship and participation with those who commit sinful and immoral acts?

7. What does it mean to be righteous and holy? What do we need to do to keep practicing righteousness and holiness?

8. Since two thousand years have passed without Christ's return, what encouragement does the promise, "I come quickly" give us?

9. Is it easy to dismiss Hell—the lake burning with fire and brimstone as a super-spiritual myth. What does the book add to our understanding of the reality of Hell and the possibility of being eternally separated from God?

10. The letters were written to encourage Christians facing impending persecution. What encouragement can contemporary Christians take from them as well as the concluding chapter of Revelation?

DAILY DEVOTIONAL READING:

DAY 1 - Habakkuk 2:1-3

DAY 4 - Daniel 7

DAY 5 - Ezekiel 37

DAY 2 - Matthew 13

DAY 3 - Matthew 17: 1-9

DAY 6 - John 4:5-28

DAY 7 - Acts 28

===

Glossary

Antipas
The traditional account says that John the Apostle ordained Antipas as bishop of Pergamon during the reign of the Roman emperor Nero and that he was martyred during the reign of Nero, by burning in a brazen bull-shaped altar for casting out demons worshiped by the local population.

Apocalypse
Judeo-Christian writings of 200 B.C.E. to 150 C.E. marked by symbolic imagery, and the expectation of an imminent cosmic cataclysmic event in which God destroys the ruling powers of evil and raises the righteous to life in a messianic kingdom

Apostle
One who is sent by God with authority to preach the gospel either as the first prominent missionary to a region or to give direction to and exercise moral and spiritual influence over other leaders.

Asia Minor
The western extremity of Asia roughly equivalent to the Asian part of modern Turkey

Balaam
The Old Testament prophet who disobeyed God's urgings not to meet with Balak or curse the Israelites. In the II Peter, he exemplifies one who denied the faith for the sake of material gain.

Balak
The Old Testament king of Moab who was fearful of the Israelites because of what they had done to the Amorites and hired Balaam to curse them.

Gnosticism
Belief or conviction that matter (including the physical body) is evil and that emancipation from evil comes through secret spiritual knowledge that is essential to salvation.

Heresy
The denial of biblically revealed truth and any belief that is contrary to orthodox Christian doctrine.

Jezebel
The Phoenician wife of King Ahab of Israel. According to the account in I and II Kings, she opposed the prophet Elijah and attempted to force the Israelites to worship the false gods of Baal and Asherah. She represents an impudent, shameless, or morally unrestrained woman.

Key of David
The Spiritual authority within the Kingdom of God that is given to believers because of their relationship with Christ.

Manna
Food that was miraculously supplied to the Israelites in their journey through the wilderness. Denotes divinely supplied spiritual nourishment.

Nicolaitans
A heretical early sect believed to have been founded by Nicolas of Antioch, one of the seven men chosen to serve the Jerusalem congregation but who later embraced Gnosticism. The group believed that the human body was evil and only the spirit was good and, therefore, a Christian could do whatever he or she desired with their body. This teaching enticed many to live in unrestrained indulgence.

Made in the USA
Columbia, SC
09 March 2024

32337817R00074